GRUESOME
TALES
FROM
NORTHUMBRIA

NORTHERN
HERITAGE

First published in Great Britain by Sandhill Press Limited in 1994 as
'Body in the Bank: Famous Northern Murders'.
Selected and retold by Hazel Reynolds and editorial staff at Sandhill Press Limited.
Reprinted by Northern Heritage Services Limited 2011 and 2018.

ISBN: 9780955540684

Cover design, Ian Scott Design
Illustrations © Chloe Rodam 2011

Published by:
Northern Heritage
Unit 7 New Kennels, Blagdon Estate, Seaton Burn
Tyne & Wear NE13 6DB
Tel: 01670 789940

See our full online catalogue at: www.northern-heritage.co.uk

Printed by Martin's the Printers,
Berwick upon Tweed, UK.

CONTENTS

THE BODY
IN THE BANK

This particularly hideous murder took place at the beginning of December 1838, the chief protagonists in the events being Archibald Bolam and Joseph Millie. The two men were employed as actuary and clerk respectively in the Savings Bank situated at the entrance to the Royal Arcade, Newcastle upon Tyne.

Archibald Bolam, 41, had begun his career as a schoolmaster and through the intervention of carefully cultivated influential friends, finally rose to the responsible position he held at the time of these events. He was living at No. 2 Sedgewick Place, Union Lane, Gateshead with his housekeeper, Mary Ann Walker.

Investigations carried out after the crime revealed Bolam as something of a 'Jekyll and Hyde' character. Outwardly trustworthy and straight forward, and professing religious beliefs, it became clear that he was in fact a hypocrite of the worst kind, who kept company with *filthy and depraved characters.* Perhaps because of this he had quarrelled with many of his earlier Presbyterian friends. However, as shall be seen later, he was still not without influence with those in authority.

Joseph Millie's life, in contrast, had been one of struggle and hardship. Born in North Shields, his father's ironmongery business went bankrupt and he was forced to sell all he possessed to pay the creditors. By the time of the events related here, he was 56 years old, married, and scratching a living by working as an occasional clerk at the bank.

The story begins early in 1838 when a much respected gentleman, Mr. George Ridley, was appointed as the assistant clerk to Archibald Bolam. At first the two men got on well together, but gradually Bolam seemed to turn against his colleague, to the extent of trying to lose him his job. This he succeeded in doing in December of the same year, and Millie, to whom Bolam seemed to have taken a liking, was appointed to the post. Alas for Millie! it must have appeared to him that at last luck was on his side, and life would be much easier with a full time job and wage.

Only two days later, and Millie was dead - murdered with *"revolting brutality."*

The alarm was raised when a servant employed in a shop adjoining the bank, noticed smoke pouring from the building. It was approximately 2.00a.m. on 7th December. The police and fire brigade were summoned immediately.

Entering through the waiting room, the firemen forced the door to Bolam's office, which appeared to be the seat of the fire. Almost blinded by the black, acrid smoke, they stumbled across something heavy lying on the floor. Lanterns were brought and they illuminated a scene of sickening violence.

Face down on the hearthrug in a pool of blood, lay the body of the unfortunate grey-haired clerk. All around him were traces of a terrible death struggle. At least twenty wounds had been inflicted on him, his skull smashed in places, left jaw and cheekbone broken. The hearthrug was saturated with blood and brains and the surrounding furniture and walls were splattered with the same hideous gore.

Close to the victim's feet were a set of fire-irons, possibly dropped after an ineffectual attempt at self-defence. At his side lay a poker covered with blood and hair - the murder weapon. The pockets of Millie's coat were found to contain coals and paper, and it began to appear that a deliberate attempt had been made to start the fire as a cover-up to the crime.

But what had become of Archibald Bolam? A further search revealed him, slumped in a corner of the room, apparently unconscious. He seemed to be suffering from the effects of smoke, and a slight wound to the throat.

5

Almost at once however, the suspicion arose that he was only *"shamming"* concussion, as his eyes seemed *"clear and bright."* A small quantity of blood was found on his desk together with a blood-stained paper knife - possibly used to inflict the scratch wound on his throat. Bolam was taken to the house of a chemist, Mr. Glenton, and examined there by Drs. Nesham and Walker, but no serious injury was found.

Later the same day, Bolam related his extraordinary tale to the magistrates, Mr. Aldermann Dunn and Mr. Woods. First he claimed to have been receiving threatening letters. Then he stated he had returned to the bank from home, entered his office and seeing Millie lying on the hearthrug, assumed he was asleep! Crossing to his desk, he was suddenly confronted by a man with a blackened face, who struck him a blow to the right temple. Although he broke away and tried to shout for help from the window, he was again attacked and struck to the ground. His assailant then tried to cut his throat.

An inquest was opened on the unfortunate Millie the same afternoon at the Blue Posts, Pilgrim Street. The packed inn heard Bolam repeat his incredible story to hoots of derision. Very quickly a verdict of 'Wilful Murder' was returned, and Bolam was taken into custody and committed for trial at the Spring Assizes in the following March.

Such a foul murder stirred an ugly tide of opinion against the prisoner, not least because it was felt that having *"friends in high places"* would enable Bolam to escape justice. For his own protection therefore, a guard was placed around him on the journey between court and gaol. The mob lined the route howling for his hanging.

The March Assizes found against Bolam, but an application to postpone the trial to midsummer and transfer it to the county of Northumberland, was successful. The case was finally heard on 30th July 1839 by Mr. Justice Maule.

The prosecution called as their witness the bank porter. He gave evidence that he had left the bank on the afternoon before the murder at 3.30p.m. Both Bolam and Millie were then alive and well and *"sitting together like brothers."* One of Bolam's neighbours in Gateshead then stated that he had heard sounds of breaking glass as if an entry was being forced at the rear of Bolam's house that same afternoon. Mary Ann Walker, the housekeeper, was summoned, and she confirmed Bolam had returned to the house.

However she was such a shifty character and created such a very bad impression, being found out in several lies, that the Judge warned she could be charged as an accessory or accomplice. Perhaps because of this, she then admitted sponging marks from Bolam's coat sleeve. Close examination of the garment revealed bloodstains and smears.

The Prosecution's theory was that Bolam and Millie had quarrelled, and the former had beaten out the brains of his unlucky clerk in a frenzied attack. Having attempted, with the help of Walker, to remove the signs of the fight from his person, he returned to the bank and set the fire, presumably hoping that Millie's body would be destroyed. He had also prepared a story for the police of an unknown assailant should his plan go wrong. It seemed the action of a desperate man, for he could, of course, have perished himself in the fire.

On the question of motive, no evidence was given at all, although the Prosecution undoubtedly attempted to 'suggest' possible solutions to this point to the jury. The defence, conducted by Mr. Dundas with a masterly display of eloquence, also made much of the lack of a motive.

The jury however, accepted the theory of a quarrel and fight, but Mr. Justice Maule summed up so favourably for the prisoner, that he was reprieved from hanging, and sentenced to be transported for life. Local feelings were so inflamed by this verdict, that Bolam was lucky to escape the attentions of a lynch mob.

Many years later in 1889 through correspondence reported in the Newcastle Weekly Chronicle, it was revealed that Bolam had protested his innocence until death. An inscription on his tombstone in St. Stephen's Church, Sydney was said to read as follows:

The writer to the paper was a Sydney gentleman, Mr. Reynolds, who claimed to have sifted carefully through all the evidence and talked to Bolam himself. Speaking of the motive for the crime, which remained the biggest mystery, Mr. Reynolds said: *"It was a terrible story; if not the worst I have heard, certainly the worst for many years, and sufficiently sickening to bury."*

So the case remained a puzzle, although people who had known Bolam in Australia talked of a miniature of a lady that he kept close to his heart, suggesting perhaps that it had been a crime of passion. Whatever the motive, it can not be assumed that Bolam was innocent, and without doubt the unfortunate Millie met a most horrible death.

DEATH OF
THE TAX COLLECTOR

Just over 20 years after the sensational case of 'The Body in the Bank', news of another brutal murder swept through Newcastle. This shocking attack took place in broad daylight in Blackett Street near the city centre. The victim was Mr. Mark Frater a highly respected local business man and tax collector with offices in that area.

Mr. Frater lived at Bulman's Village, Gosforth, and was the owner of the local omnibus company which ran from there to Grey's Monument. On the fateful morning of 1st October 1861, he had left home as usual at 9.00a.m. and travelled to work by bus to Northumberland Street. Here he was seen by several witnesses as he alighted from the bus and began his walk to his office at the end of Blackett Street.

Reaching his office door, he paused briefly to speak to a friend, and while they chatted, a man, later identified as George Clark, suddenly grabbed him from behind and savagely stabbed him in the throat. The dreadful force of the blow gashed across Mark's cheek, and glancing off his jaw bone, plunged deep into his neck, where it severed all the main arteries.

The crazed attacker deliberately wrenched the knife around in the wound to such an extent that the blade was completely twisted out of shape. He then calmly withdrew the weapon from Mark's body and stood gazing triumphantly at his unfortunate victim.

In deep shock, and scarely able to comprehend what had happened, Mark opened the door to his office and staggered inside. Collapsing into a chair, he groaned to his astonished clerk, *"I'm afraid I'm done for,"* and then slumped in a dead faint across his desk. Blood from the dreadful wound

9

poured down his body and flowed across the papers on the desk top. Although a doctor was immediately summoned, within ten minutes of the ferocious attack, Mark Frater was dead.

Outside, George Clark was held captive by two passers-by, Mr. McGill and Mr. Dalrymple, until he could be handed over to the officers of the law. He appeared calm and composed and made no attempt to try and escape. Indeed when he was brought before the magistrates the next day, he readily admitted his guilt saying, *"Decidedly so, decidedly so; I've murdered him; he robbed me, and now I've robbed him."*
He then added, *"This is a grand job for the penny papers; they'll have a rare sale today."*

Further questioning revealed that Clark held a deep grudge against Mark Frater in his capacity of tax collector. One of the taxes for which Mark was responsible was the dog tax and Clark owned a dog! He had refused to pay the tax due for six months and had therefore served a period of imprisonment for the offence. For this he held Mark Frater personally responsible and had therefore taken his terrible revenge.

At the ensuing Assizes the case was simply proved and Clark was convicted of the murder and sentenced to be hung. In fact, because of his obvious mental state, he was reprieved on the grounds of insanity, and confined to an asylum for the rest of his life.

THE
MATFEN MURDER

News of the vicious murder of Dorothy Bewicke swept quickly through the peaceful village of Matfen in the autumn of 1855. Well-known and respected locally, Dorothy had worked for several years as a housekeeper and was honest, hard-working and trustworthy, being praised for her skills in cookery. Throughout her life she had been very careful with money and eventually managed to save enough to purchase some property.

Situated near Stamfordham Row, at the junction of two lanes, were the five small cottages that became Dorothy's security for life. An acre of land adjoined the buildings where she kept cows, pigs and poultry and grew grain. Unfortunately the buildings themselves were in very poor condition and Dorothy had no money left for repairs. Perhaps because of this, her tenants were rather disreputable, inclined to be unruly, often brawling and quarrelling and generally giving the place a bad name.

Dorothy's own cottage was very dilapidated, with a badly leaking roof and glass missing from every window. Odd rags and cloths were used to cover the worst holes. Her furniture was also very crude and rough, but she considered herself fortunate to have her own home.

In October of that year only three of the five cottages were inhabited. The first and largest being Dorothy's own, containing a kitchen and parlour, stairs from the kitchen leading to her bedroom. Over the parlour was another unused room to which access was gained by an outside staircase. Next to the cottage was the cow-house, the rooms above which had been occupied by a labourer, Barnard Dobbin, his wife and children, but finding them very cold and damp, the family quickly moved to the fourth house in the row.

Other tenants included Michael Leonard, a 'drainer' for a squire in Stamfordham, his wife and two children, and James Conroy and family. The Conroys also had a total of five lodgers: Michael, Jane and Elizabeth Anderson, their mother Isabella and a man named John Simm. They regularly travelled the countryside by horse and cart, selling the brooms they had made.

The end cottage in the row was often let to tramps and gypsies who the local people suspected of being poachers or worse. All in all Dorothy's tenants were disliked by the other villagers and she was often urged to give them notice. However she ignored this advice, an action which was to lead to tragedy.

On the morning of Sunday 21st October, 1855 it was discovered that Dorothy's house had been broken into, and she was found dead - cruelly murdered.

The motive appeared to be robbery as the entire cottage had been ransacked. The burglars had taken the precaution of screening all the windows with sacks and quilts to cover their deeds. Cunningly, they had also fastened the door of Dobbin's cottage with a rope or piece of halter. It had been twisted around the sneck, and then through the staple in the doorpost, to prevent the occupants leaving if the alarm was raised.

Suspicions were first aroused when Dobbin discovered this, although at that stage he merely thought that a practical joke had been played on him. His daughter went to Dorothy's house to fetch the daily milk, and found the door open, but the house in darkness, and the strange hangings at the windows.

Dobbin arrived at the house in response to his daughter's cries and pushed open the door calling, "Dolly, are you in?" There was no reply and he ran out into the road and shouted again from there. He was joined by Matthew Laing, a shoe-maker who lived at Ingo Mill nearby. Together the two men entered the cottage.

A scene of devastation awaited them. All the contents of the kitchen had been thrown around the room, drawers and cupboards emptied, and the window pane removed. Hesitating again, the men retreated into the road. At this point John Harrison, a respectable farmer from Muckleridge rode by. After hearing their story, he accompanied them back into the house.

Upstairs they discovered to their horror, the body of the old lady dead on the floor. Almost naked, her hands had been bound across her chest with a leather strap, and her feet were tied together with part of an old halter. From the marks on her throat she had obviously been strangled, her features were livid and distorted, twisted in agony. As with the kitchen, the bedroom had been ransacked, even the mattress was ripped open, presumably during the search for valuables.

At once Harrison set off on a fast horse to report the murder to the police at Bellingham, Acomb, Hexham, Corbridge, Kirkwhelpington, Blaydon and Newcastle, thereby ensuring the alarm was spread as widely as possible.

Suspicion immediately fell on Conroy and his two lodgers, John Simm and Michael Allan. The three men were arrested the same night by John Gillespie, the police superintendent at Kirkwhelpington. Conroy's wife and sisters were also arrested and questioned. No clear evidence emerged to connect them with the murder, but they were all committed for trial.

On 29th February, 1856 the prisoners were brought before a packed court at the Northumberland Assizes in the Moot Hall, Newcastle upon Tyne. Mr. Justice Willes was presiding and all the defendants pleaded "Not Guilty."

John Simm was called as a prosecution witness but added little to the largely circumstantial evidence against the prisoners. A hazel stick, with hammer head attached, and a stick of mountain ash, both newly cut, had been found in Dorothy's bedroom. They corresponded to some wood cuttings from sticks with which the male prisoners had been

13

seen in Sweethope Dene, near Kirkwhelpington, a few days before the murder.

A halter was found in their house, believed to be part of the same one used to fasten Dobbin's door, and to secure the unfortunate victim's legs. It appeared that the leather strap used to bind her arms could also have come from the same source, as Michael Allan had been seen wearing a similar strap, which was missing on his arrest.

In a field near to the cottage where the defendants had been recently observed, three silver spoons belonging to the deceased were discovered. Evidence was also given that one of the female prisoners, Isabella Allan, had borrowed a candle and lucifer matches from Patrick O'Callaghan at West Harle. These items had been noticed lying in the kitchen and both the victim's body and bedroom floor were spattered with candle grease.

Although all this evidence pointed towards the guilt of the prisoners, the jury acquitted them, to the delight of the watching crowd. Much was made of the fact that Dorothy had repeatedly been warned about the potential danger of some of her disreputable tenants. Sir Edward Blackett had offered to buy the property to clear the area of these "vagabonds" - but Dorothy had refused to sell. It seems a cruel judgement however, to infer that she was in some way responsible for her hideous fate.

Not long after the Matfen murder, Michael Allan was convicted with another man of a brutal garotte robbery at North Shields. At this trial it was revealed by Mr. Dunne, the Chief Constable of Newcastle upon Tyne, that Allan was a member of a desperate gang of thieves known to be at large in the county. Allan's luck had run out, and he was sentenced to be transported for life. Perhaps therefore Dorothy's murder was at last partly avenged.

MURDERED
BY MISTAKE?

Hardly had the news of the Matfen murder been circulated, when the public were shocked by another brutal killing in their midst. This took place on 1st November, 1855 at 'Smailes Lane' now 'Stirling Lane' near Gibside Woods about one and half miles from Burnopfield, County Durham. The unfortunate victim was a young assistant surgeon, Robert Stirling, and after investigation, it appeared that he had been killed in mistake for another.

The story begins with Robert's failure to report for duty on the fateful day. He had been recently appointed as assistant to Doctor Watson at the Hall in Burnopfield, and during his short time in the practice had already won a reputation as hardworking, caring and efficient. When he was still missing the following day, Dr. Watson assumed he must have returned to Scotland to visit his parents.

He was discovered to be mistaken almost immediately however, as Robert's parents arrived to visit their son. His mother was desperately worried for his safety having had a vivid dream in which she saw her son being murdered in some woods. She claimed that she had clearly seen the faces of the killers and would be able to identify them. Hearing of Robert's absence she at once demanded that a search be made for him.

The following Tuesday, 6th November, the body was discovered by the distraught father in Smailes Wood near to Smailes Lane. It emerged that Dr. Stirling must have been shot at about mid-day on Thursday 1st November by someone lurking in the bushes at the side of the road.

Although the shot was not fatal, his cowardly assailants had also battered him about the head with the butt end of a gun, and cut his throat. His hands were found to be clasped tightly together around clumps of grass he must have torn from the ground in his agony.

A farmer working in a nearby field about noon on that day reported hearing shouts and laughter, but he had not been suspicious of such ordinary sounds. It seems that the murderers had been 'enjoying' their task and covering any cries for help uttered by their unfortunate victim. They had robbed the body of money, a watch and ring, and also taken the doctor's bag of surgical instruments. There had then been some attempt to conceal the crime by dragging the body into the woods.

No one could understand the motive in killing the young affable doctor who had so recently moved to the district and seemed to have no enemies. At this stage it began to look like a case of mistaken identity. It was discovered that John Errington, a farmer and keeper of the Bute Arms at High Spen, had been expected to pass down Smailes Lane about noon on the day of the murder, on his way to pay his rent to Mr. John Bowles at Gibside Hall. It seemed probable that he could have been the intended victim, the motive being robbery. There was also a superficial resemblance in appearance to Dr. Stirling.

This theory so shocked and saddened John Errington that he suffered a nervous breakdown, and refused to go out after dark. Indeed, he never really recovered his health and died not long after.

Searches now began for the perpetrators of this dreadful murder and huge rewards were offered for information. Several men were arrested on suspicion and two of them were identified by Mrs. Stirling from her dream. They were John Kane, also known as 'Whisky Jack' (*see our book entitled: 'Rogues and Reivers of the North Country'*), and Richard Rayne, a blacksmith from Winlaton.

They were brought up before Justice Baron Martin at the Spring Assizes in Durham in 1856, but as the evidence presented was not considered sufficiently convincing, they

16

were remanded in custody until the Summer Assizes.

On the 25th and 26th of July the trial was held before Mr. Justice Willes, Mr. Overend appearing for the prosecution, Mr. Monk and Mr. Dawson for the defence. A great deal of circumstantial evidence was presented but nothing that directly tied the accused to the murder, although public opinion was severely against the pair.

Again the case was found not proved, and a verdict of "Not Guilty" was announced. Some records of the time claim that this was largely due to the persistence of one juryman called Quaker, who was quoted as insisting that "there was a long chain of evidence, but not one sound link."

Inevitably suspicion existed locally that the men were guilty, or how had Dr. Stirling's mother identified them so positively? It was also suggested that Quaker had been bribed by the defence, and several other rumours circulated about a gang of robbers.

Nothing further was ever discovered about the case however, and Kane and Rayne were free to go on with their lives while the body of the promising young surgeon, only 26 years old, was laid to rest in the churchyard at Tanfield. A memorial was erected there by his grieving parents, and for many years the grave was lovingly tended by his patients.

THE
POISONED SYRINGE

Of all the dreadful methods used by those who commit murder, poison, particularly when administered over a period of time, is perhaps the most abhorrent. This slow, silent killer does its deadly work unknown to the victim, who is watched intently by the poisoner for the fateful signs of approaching death.

In 1855 one such case, the death of Jane Wooler at Burdon near Darlington, aroused passionate public feelings against the accused, her husband, Joseph Snaith Wooler. The sensational trial that followed was reported in grim detail in the local and national press, and discussed throughout the length and breadth of the country.

Suspicions were initially expressed by Dr. Jackson and Dr. Hazeldene who had attended Jane during her long and puzzling illness. She had suffered dreadfully in the weeks and months before her death, and all the treatments and medicines given had proved ineffective.

After the body was ordered exhumed, a post mortem found arsenic present in sufficient quantities to have caused death. The evidence further pointed to the poison having been given in small doses over a long period of time. The doctors claimed that this accounted for their being unable to diagnose their patient's illness, or treat it successfully.

Jane's husband was arrested and charged with her murder. It was revealed that he had up to thirty different kinds of poison in his house. Branded a heartless monster by his neighbours and the general public, it seemed that nothing could save Wooler from the scaffold.

It soon appeared however that the case was not to have such a foregone conclusion. For the considerable sum of

£2,000, Joseph Wooler retained for his defence the colourful and charismatic light of the English legal service, Serjeant Wilkins. Slightly disreputable with a mysterious background, even allegedly the illegitimate son of Lord Shaftesbury, Wilkins had a string of successful cases behind him. He was assisted by Mr. Overend and Mr. Lawrie; Edward James, Leofrie Temple and Mr. Dawson appearing for the prosecution.

The trial began before Justice Baron Martin in the final month of 1855, opening with the considerable medical evidence which had been amassed against the defendant. Reported in macabre detail in the Newcastle Journal of 15th December, the most damning parts concerned the arsenic found in the body's organs, and the traces of the same poison discovered in the syringe used for injections given to Jane by her husband.

In a dramatic counter attack the defence were able to prove that the infected syringe had been kept in a drawer with others by which it could have been contaminated. Hectored by Wilkins, Drs. Jackson and Hazeldene were forced to admit that they had not suspected arsenic poisoning until after death, and the defence drew the conclusion that they had panicked and acted to protect their reputations. It was a commonly held belief at that time that death was often due to medical incompetence!

A masterly summing up by the defence slammed the prosecution's inability to produce a single witness to prove that Wooler had behaved badly towards his wife. In fact they were able to show him as a caring and thoughtful husband, due chiefly to the evidence given by his servant, Ann Taylor. Wilkins' passionate and graphic description of Wooler's devotion to Jane during the worst bouts of her illness aroused considerable sympathy in the court. The climax of his speech occurred when Wooler, who throughout the trial had appeared calm and unemotional, seemed to be suddenly overcome by his feelings, and fainted in the dock.

Amazed at the contrast to the prisoner's earlier

controlled behaviour, the jury believed him to be genuinely suffering real anguish at the events revealed in court, and felt very compassionate towards him. These feelings were added to by the Judge in his summary making the following comments: *"the law requires not suspicion only, but plain and natural consequences, not far fetched ones, from the evidence. It is for you to say that the prisoner administered the arsenic, I am unable to."* Not surprisingly, within ten minutes a verdict of "Not Guilty" was returned.

Dismissing the case against the accused, Judge Martin hinted darkly that: *"I may observe that, if I were to make a surmise, there is a person upon whom my fancy would rest rather than the prisoner."* Together with the acquittal, these remarks caused a furore in the press, and the Judge became nervous and tried to deny what he had said.

Rumours increased, and suggestions were made that Ann Taylor, the servant, had been involved in the crime, with Wooler's sister. Several present in court during the trial declared that the Judge had been staring at the two doctors when he made his controversial remarks. The Newcastle Journal took up the debate, and it was revealed that a year before Jane's death, another female patient of Dr. Jackson died mysteriously, and arsenic was suggested as the cause at the inquest. The newspaper then wrote an article directing the two doctors to keep a more watchful eye on the mixing of drugs and the use of syringes. Furious, the doctors replied and a war of words raged through the press reaching the columns of the Times.

The publicity was shortlived, as a few days later news of the murder of more than eight people claimed the headlines. By then the reputations of the two doctors were destroyed and they were forced to give up their practices. Joseph Wooler however enjoyed a quiet retirement.

THE BELANEY
POISONING CASE

Although this controversial murder took place in London in 1844, the characters and the background leading up to it can be traced back to the small village of North Sunderland, near Seahouses, on the Northumberland coast.

Mrs. Skelly, a widow, had lived in the village for many years, together with her beautiful daughter, Rachel. The girl had many admirers but did not fall in love until a young doctor, James Cockburn Belaney, arrived in the area from across the Border.

Seeking his fortune, he settled in the village and, although he was not properly licensed, set up a practice. Belaney was said to have a "lively" personality, and to be interested in botany, ornithology, old sports and history. He tried to interest his neighbours and the village folk in his passion for falconry, but did not succeed in endearing himself to the local people.

He did, however, successfully woo the lovely Rachel and they were married in February 1843. The doctor then gave up his practice, which was not particularly lucrative, and proceeded to administer his mother-in-law's business affairs. Mrs. Skelly owned lands from the Bamburgh Trust and had interests in mines and the local industry of lime kilning.

Not long after Belaney's move into her house, Mrs. Skelly died, according to her son-in-law, from a bilious fever. (He later changed his diagnosis, as we shall see.)

Three months later the couple went to the court at Bamburgh and were jointly admitted as the inheritors of the widow's land, with Rachel maintaining the overall control for a short while until she made a will in favour of Belaney.

He proved to be a model husband and an agreeable

neighbour. No harsh words were heard between the couple and they seemed happy together as Belaney enjoyed his new role of gentleman, administering to the business affairs of his wife's estate.

In 1844, when his wife was fairly well advanced in pregnancy, Belaney decided to take her to London for *"a glimpse of fashionable life."* He planned to see friends there and to meet up with the Duke of Leeds to arrange a visit to the Prince of Netherlands concerning exhibitions of falconry on the Rhine. Before leaving he suggested they should both make a will, joking that no one should visit London without doing so, *"in case of accidents"*. The wills were dated 31st May 1844 and business matters were left in the hands of the steward, Mr. Bell.

The couple arrived at the Euston Hotel on 3rd June but left for other lodgings at 48 Green Street Stepney, the following day. Belaney was beginning to act suspiciously as he wrote to his steward a couple of days later implying that he was still staying at the Euston Hotel. In his letter he suggested that his wife was unwell after the journey and a miscarriage was threatened. Mrs Belaney was, in fact, perfectly well and the couple visited the theatre on 4th June and did some sightseeing for the next few days.

Having lived in the East End for some five or six years previously, the small circle of friends to whom Belaney introduced his wife included Mr. Hobson, a bookseller, and Mr. Donoghue, a chemist. Mr. Hobson later claimed that Belaney had once shown him a phial of poison he kept hidden in a drawer.

Belaney visited Donoghue on 5th June and asked for some prussic acid, claiming he had heart trouble. The chemist knew Belaney was a doctor and gave him the poison together with various simple drugs such as salts and senna. A 'black draught' was later purchased on 6th June.

Until 8th June the visit had been going well, but on this day Mrs. Belaney complained of feeling ill. The evidence later given at the trial describes the following sequence of events.

At 8.a.m. that morning a servant girl was cleaning the room next to Mrs. Belaney's and heard the couple talking quite normally. Shortly afterwards, having returned downstairs, she heard Belaney cry out in alarm for the landlady, Mrs. Heppingstall.

Running upstairs, she found Mrs. Belaney clenching her teeth and foaming at the mouth and she asked Belaney if his wife was having a fit. He replied that it was heart disease, and his mother-in-law had died with the same symptoms nine months previously.

The landlady was anxious to call a doctor but Belaney pointed out that he was a doctor himself. Ignoring this, Mrs. Heppingstall sent the servant for another doctor, still feeling that a second opinion was essential.

As they waited Belaney implied that he did not think his wife would survive and repeated the story of his mother-in-law's death. He suggested putting a pan of hot water at his wife's feet, later moving it to warm her hands.

The doctor, a Mr. Garnett, arrived too late - Mrs. Belaney gasped her last breath and died. Belaney repeated his story about the heart disease to Mr. Garnett and said that his wife had taken only salts. The doctor agreed that the symptoms tied in with Belaney's explanation but insisted that an inquest be carried out.

This was held on 10th June and the court was told that a pint of prussic acid was found in the victim's stomach at the post mortem. Later that day Belaney visited Mr. Garnett and confessed to having bought the prussic acid for his own heart condition. He then explained the dreadful events as follows.

On the morning of his wife's death, he had broken the neck of the poison bottle while trying to open it. He poured the contents into a glass and went into the other room to get another bottle. He had apparently been delayed writing letters, and his wife, having got up to take some salts, wanted to remove their taste and drank off the prussic acid assuming the

23

colourless liquid was water. According to Belaney, she immediately said, "*Oh, I have taken that hot stuff, give me some water.*" When asked why he had not mentioned these facts before, Belaney claimed to be ashamed of his carelessness.

The inquest resulted in a verdict of wilful murder and the trial took place on 21st August. The chief points made by the prosecution were that Belaney had given contradictory accounts about the cause of death of his mother-in-law. Also, his wife would not have been able to speak after taking such a large dose of prussic acid - large enough to kill. It was unlikely that any doctor would have tried to revive a patient by placing warm water on the hands and feet.

The strongest evidence came from the letters Belaney sent to his steward, Mr. Bell, in North Sunderland. He had dated some from the Euston Hotel when he was, in fact, staying in Stepney. He wrote on the fatal day, 8th June, that he had moved his wife to different lodgings, where she was attended by two doctors, as she was dangerously ill having gone into premature labour. Belaney again suggested that one of the doctor's had mentioned heart disease in connection with Mrs. Belaney's condition. On the day of her death, he wrote to Mr. Bell, "*Rachel is no more.*"

The motive for his wife's murder, was that Belaney would inherit property worth about seven or eight thousand pounds.

The defence stated that Belaney and his wife were on good terms, and a Dr. Embleton from Northumberland gave evidence saying that he had prescribed prussic acid to Belaney for, among other things, dyspesia. One witness told of Mrs. Belaney shopping in Regent Street, buying a pattern and the necessary materials to embroider a falcon. She intended to give the present to her husband on his return from Europe. The contradictions in Belaney's statement were attributed partly to confusion, and partly to his fear of being blamed for carelessness. This was, according to a 'friend', one of the doctor's characteristics while in medical practice.

The judge summed up, again pointing out the contradictions in Belaney's evidence and after consulting for an hour, the jury returned a verdict of 'Not Guilty'. Belaney heaved a sigh of relief, but others were astounded by the verdict.

Belaney soon returned to North Sunderland but found that public opinion was against him, and, as he entered his house, angry villagers gathered in threatening groups. On Saturday 16th September, three men dressed in women's clothes, their faces blackened, accompanied by five hundred jeering local people paraded an effegy hoisted on poles through the local streets.

When the crowd drew opposite Belaney's house, he rushed out and fired into the mass of local people. It was not known if the weapon was loaded, but the crowd seethed towards him and the pistol was dropped. It was later retrieved by someone and used to smash the windows in Belaney's house, the doors and gates were broken and most of the furniture was destroyed.

Matters reached a climax on the 18th September when Belaney's house was set on fire and looted by the crowd. He escaped to Alnwick but was recognised in the Willow Tree Inn by a group who blackmailed him for drinking money.

Special sessions were held at Belford on 7th October to enquire into charges about the fire brought by Belaney against his steward, Mr. Bell, and others. The doctor's brother, Rev. Robert Belaney gave a rousing account of the assault and destruction of property.

The evidence implicating Bell was that he was seen drunk in a public house saying that there would be "a farce at the Sunk Fence that night". The enquiry lasted two days and the magistrate decided no suspicion rested on Bell or the others. Shortly afterwards Belaney disappeared from North Sunderland and was never seen again.

MARY ANN COTTON

"Mary Ann Cotton
She's dead and she's rotten
She lies in her bed
With eyes wide open
Sing, sing, oh, what can I sing
Mary Ann Cotton is tied up with string.
Where, where? Up in the air
Sellin' black puddens a penny a pair."

Childrens rhyme.

The name of Mary Ann Cotton is still heard through the rhymes and sayings of the north east of England, particularly in County Durham. This notorious female poisoner, thought to have murdered between fifteen and twenty people, is now a part of our folklore.

Born around 1832 in the pit village of Low Moorsley in the parish of Houghton-le-Spring, Mary Ann Robson, as she was then, was said to have been a pretty child with dark eyes. Her father was a pitman, and her mother, having married young, had three children before she was twenty years old.

When she was sixteen Mary Ann began work as a nursemaid, and these early years were happy and trouble free. She married her first husband, William Mowbray, a labourer at Murton pit, in July 1852 at St. Andrew's church, Newcastle. Shortly after the marriage the couple moved south to the Plymouth area, where Mary Ann had four children, three of whom died while she was away from home. There is little evidence at this stage to suspect foul play, as infant mortality was rife in the nineteenth century. On her return north five years later, Mary Ann brought the remaining child, a girl called Mary Ann, back with her. Four children were born to the couple after their return to County Durham. In 1860 the child brought from Plymouth died and by 1864 two of the other children were also dead. All were diagnosed as having gastric fever, as was Mowbray himself who died in 1865, and all were insured with the British and Prudential Insurance Company.

Following these events, Mary Ann worked as a nurse at Sunderland and married a former patient, Geordie Ward, who died the next year after a lingering and perplexing illness. She then became housekeeper to widower James Robinson, a shipyard worker, whom she married six months later. Before the marriage, however, two of Robinson's children died, and around the same time Mowbray's remaining child, Isabella, met her fate. She had been living with Mary Ann's mother who died after being nursed by her daughter (again suspicions were not aroused). Isabella and Robinson's children had all suffered similar symptoms - foaming at the mouth, tossing around in bed and severe sickness, particularly after being given a drink by Mary Ann.

Mary Ann gave birth to Robinson's child in 1867, but the baby died after a few days, apparently another victim of gastric fever. Two of Robinson's other children and a second child she had to him, miraculously survived this catalogue of death and disaster. Robinson, not suprisingly, became suspicious of Mary Ann and refused to allow her to insure him. When she later ran up bad debts, they quarrelled and she left him.

She met her fourth husband, Frederick Cotton, who lived at North Walbottle, in 1870, having been introduced to him by her friend Margaret, Cotton's sister. After the death of Cotton's first wife, Mary Ann visited the household and may have stayed for a while. Conveniently, Margaret died after suffering severe stomach pains at a time when Mary Ann was already pregnant by Cotton.

27

Committing bigamy, as she was still married to Robinson, Mary Ann eventually married Cotton later that year at St. Andrew's church and their child was born in the following January. Never having settled in North Walbottle, Mary Ann moved, together with Cotton and two of his boys, to West Auckland.

Her main reason for moving there, unknown to Cotton, was that her old friend and lover, Joseph Nattrass, lived in the same street and worked at the same colliery as her new husband. Two months later when Frederick died, apparently from gastric fever, Nattrass came to live with Mary Ann and it was assumed they would marry.

However about this time Mary Ann was asked to take care of a Mr. Quick Manning, an excise officer at a local brewery. He too seems to have fallen for her charms and they talked of marriage. Disaster struck again as, within the three weeks from 10th March to 1st April, Cotton's eldest son, Frederick, died, as did her own baby Robert and the lodger, Nattrass. Frederick and Nattrass were said to have died from the fever, whilst the baby died during teething.

By this time Mary Ann was carrying Mr. Quick Manning's child and she moved house taking the remaining boy, Charles Edward Cotton, with her. Several weeks went by without any sign of her marrying the excise officer, and although she had been left money by both Cotton and Nattrass, she began to resent the expense of keeping the child.

On Saturday 6th July she told Mr. Riley, the assistant overseer and local shopkeeper, that the child was *"in the way"*, and that she had asked the boy's uncle to take him to Ipswich. He had refused and Mary Ann asked Riley to put Charles Edward in the workhouse. Riley said that she would have to accompany the boy and she replied "Perhaps it won't matter, as I won't be troubled long. He'll go like all the rest of the Cotton family."

By the 12th July the boy was dead and Riley became suspicious, informing the local police and the doctor, Kilburn.

28

Having visited the boy throughout the week, the doctor was surprised to learn of his death. When Riley voiced his suspicions, Kilburn refused to issue a death certificate and a post mortem was carried out followed by an inquest on 13th July. Death was found to be from natural causes, but the Newcastle Journal picked up the story and rumours of poisoning began to spread.

Mr. Quick Manning suddenly disappeared from the scene and Mary Ann prepared to leave West Auckland. She would undoubtedly have gone sooner if she had known that Dr. Kilburn had retained the boy's stomach and its contents after the post mortem, as he had not had enough time to examine them properly. When he was able to carry out closer chemical tests, he found evidence of arsenic and informed the police.

On the 18th July Mary Ann Cotton was arrested and charged with the murder of Charles Edward Cotton. A search for evidence in the house was made, without success. Permission was granted from the Home Office to exhume the child's body and the coffin was dug up on 26th July. Further examination revealed arsenic in the bowels, liver and other organs. By Wednesday 21st August, Mary Ann Cotton faced a charge of wilful murder.

A neighbour, Mrs. Dodds, gave evidence that while she was helping Mary Ann to clean the house some six weeks earlier, Charles was sent to the chemist for arsenic and soft soap in order to kill bed bugs. The chemist refused to serve the boy and Mrs. Dodds collected the mixture, half of which was used, the rest put away in a pint jug. This evidence together with Dr. Kilburn's post mortem findings and Riley's report of Mary Ann wanting to be rid of the boy, resulted in her being committed for trial at the next Durham Assizes.

On 5th September permission was given to exhume Nattrass's body and again traces of arsenic were found. The bodies of the two other children were also exhumed, but officials were unable to find that of their father, Frederick

Cotton. In Durham gaol on 10th January 1873, Mary Ann Cotton gave birth to her twelfth and final child.

The trial began on 21st February at Bishop Auckland and several people lined the route as the prisoner was taken by train from the gaol. The charge of the wilful murder of Joseph Nattrass was taken up first. Two weeks before he died, Nattrass complained to workmates of feeling unwell. Mary Ann insisted on nursing him herself, giving him tea from two teapots she kept by the bedside. The doctor gave his forensic evidence and Mary Ann was committed for trial at Durham for murder.

In the case of young Frederick Cotton she was again seen to have given him drinks from the teapots but no food. Examination of the exhumed body revealed evidence of arsenic poisoning. Similar facts were put forward concerning the death of her own child by Cotton. The baby had shown signs of improvement but suddenly took a turn for the worse.

Mary Ann Cotton was committed for trial at Durham Assizes on 5th March where the only case to be heard was that of Charles Edward Cotton. The prisoner was brought into the courtroom shortly before ten o'clock : *"she looked care-worn, depressed, pale and much older..."*

The facts of the case were given again and local witnesses called. The counsel for the prosecution summed up the evidence drawing attention to the findings of the other post mortems on victims and the apparent ill-treatment of the child prior to his death.

The defence was conducted by Mr. Campbell Foster, the main thrust of his argument being that there was no direct evidence to show that the prisoner had administered the poison. Mrs. Cotton's motives were also questioned. Why should she poison Nattrass when he was earning good wages and was willing to marry her? What possible motive could she have for murdering her own baby of fourteen months? After all, she had nursed him and sent for the doctor. Was it possible that the victims were accidently poisoned as the arsenic used on the beds could still be in the air to be swallowed and inhaled?

The judge asked the jury to consider these points, but stressed in his summing up that the accidental death of four people in succession seemed beyond the bounds of coincidence and probability? Taking less than an hour, the jury returned a unanimous verdict of 'Guilty'. Standing in the dock, Mary Ann Cotton was sentenced to death by hanging on 24th March 1873. She almost fainted with shock.

Mary Ann rose early at four o'clock on the fateful day and fervently repeated her prayers. About two dozen reporters had arrived to witness the event. Sobbing and supported by two female warders, the prisoner approached the gallows. She was shaking uncontrollably and uttering prayers as the noose was placed around her neck. When the floor fell away her body swung and jerked, refusing to give up life for about three minutes. Two hundred or so people, waiting outside the prison, saw the black flag raised as they heard the drop. The body hung for an hour, and after an inquest, was buried near the west wall of the prison.

Mary Ann Cotton never confessed to her crimes. It is possible that she may have murdered twenty one people: eight of Mowbray's children, Mowbray himself, her mother, George Ward, three of Robinson's children as well as the first of her own to him, Cotton and his sister, his two children and the one she bore him, and finally, Nattrass. In reality the figure is thought to be nearer fifteen, as some of the children may well have died from natural causes.

It is unlikely that Mary Ann Cotton could have escaped the gallows, although many petitions were put forward on her behalf. Her defence counsel was inadequate, and the feeling of the time concerning the scandalous events of several marriages, bigamy and numerous suspicious deaths was definitely against her.

MURDER AT
HALLGARTH MILL

On the Sunday evening of 8th August in 1830, a young serving girl, Mary Ann Westerhope, was found brutally murdered at Hallgarth Mill, about three miles from Durham. Her throat had been cut from ear to ear, and she had also suffered a blow to the temple with a heavy implement, possibly a poker.

The mill owners, a Mr. and Mrs. Oliver, were away visiting friends and had left Mary Ann and a fellow servant, Thomas Clarke aged about nineteen, alone at the mill. The building stood a little apart from the other dwellings in the small hamlet, about three quarters of a mile from Sherburn and Pittington.

The alarm was raised at around six o'clock on the fateful day when Thomas Clarke, in a distressed and dishevelled state, appeared at the house of Thomas Addison in Sherburn. His story was that six Irishmen, dressed in sailors jackets and canvas trousers, stopped at the Mill and asked permission to light their pipes. They entered the house, but on seeing Mary Ann immediately began to attack the poor girl.

According to Clarke, one of the men first struck her in the face with his fist, another seized a large knife and, as the others held her, slashed at her throat with the weapon.

"The blood immediately fell out, she fell back, said nothing, but breathed hard."

The men then advanced on Clarke, one of them brandishing a poker. He had managed to ward off their blows, but in doing so his face was grazed causing a nose bleed. Trying to escape upstairs, he was grabbed again but fortunately his shirt gave way in the hands of his attacker, and Clarke was able to get away. The men pursued him a short way across the fields but gave up as he reached Sherburn.

Hurriedly providing Clarke with water to drink and clean his face, Addison, together with a crowd of villagers, made for the mill where they found Mary Ann's multilated body in the kitchen. Clarke was asked to ride to Durham to summon the police and doctor, but he claimed his stomach hurt as a result of the beating he had received, and therefore it was Addison himself who set off to inform the authorities.

On a closer examination, the house was found to have been ransacked and a locked drawer, containing two sovereigns and some silver, smashed open with a crow bar. The money had disappeared, but later it was found in a nearby cornfield - possibly to be retrieved when the panic had died down.

Blood stained clothing belonging to Clarke was also found which he claimed was due to the nose bleed he had suffered.

The local people were all questioned by the police, but no-one had seen or heard of any Irishmen in the area. In fact several witnesses who were near the mill around six o'clock saw nothing suspicious. Four men were later arrested at Houghton-le-Spring and questioned about the murder, but were able to prove that they were nowhere near the mill at the time the dreadful deed was committed.

Suspicion now inevitably began to point towards Thomas Clarke. No-one else had seen or heard the men he described to the police. The piece of metal used to force open the drawer which had contained the money, was marked with whitewash.

Clarke's own room was found to have been recently whitewashed. His personal savings contained in a box had been left untouched, and although he claimed to have fought for his life against six men, there were no marks of violence on his body. Most damaging of all, was his own blood stained clothing. Thomas Clarke was taken into custody and committed for trial at the following Spring Assizes in Durham.

The trial began on 25th February 1831, before Mr. Justice Littledale, and attracted a large crowd from Durham City and the surrounding area. When the court opened at eight o'clock, the room was soon filled to capacity as everyone strained forward to catch their first glimpse of the prisoner. Clarke appeared, smiling and composed, and made his plea of "Not Guilty" in a calm and confident voice.

Throughout the long day many witnesses were called to give evidence, the court continuing until almost ten o'clock. The judge and jury listened attentively as some youths who had passed the mill during the afternoon of 8th August testified that they had seen nothing unusual, just the two servants going about their normal work. A friend of Mary Ann's had visited the mill between one and two o'clock, and although she had not seen the prisoner, she had heard him talking to the girl.

The evidence against Clarke concerning his blood-stained clothing and torn shirt was produced. It was shown that there was no doubt that he had known where the money was hidden. In addition it was felt that had a genuine robbery taken place, the whole of the house would have been searched and Clarke's own money discovered and also stolen.

A doctor stated that there was no sign of violence on Clarke's body, apart from a small bruise on his thumb.

In his defence, Thomas Addison said that he knew the prisoner as a *"well-behaved young man and of good temper."* Apart from his own denial, that was the only plea made for Thomas Clarke.

The court adjourned until nine o'clock the following morning when the Judge summed up and directed the jury. Retiring at twelve fifteen, their verdict twenty five minutes later was delivered as "Guilty."

Thomas Clarke was sentenced by the Judge to be executed on the following Monday, 28th February 1831.

Huge crowds gathered early in front of Durham County Court to witness the execution. The prisoner appeared pale but composed and as he mounted the scaffold Clarke declared *"Gentlemen, I am innocent. I am going to suffer for another man's crime."* The cap was placed over his head and the drop fell, he hung there dead. An hour later, the body was taken down and transported to Durham Infirmary for dissection. There was to be no burial for Thomas Clarke.

This trial and execution were commemorated in a ballad which was printed in the Durham Advertiser after the events:

"Eighteen hundred three times ten,
August the eight that day -
Let not that Sunday and that year
From memory pass away.
At Hallgarth Mill near Pittington,
Was done a murder foul,
The female weak - the murd'rer strong -
No pity for her soul.
Her skull was broke, her throat was cut,
Her struggle was soon o' er,
And down she fell and fetched a sign,
And welter'd in her gore.
Her fellow servant, Thomas Clarke,
To Sherburn slowly sped,
And told a tale that strangers six
Had done the dreadful deed.
Now, woe betide thee, Thomas Clarke!
For this thy coward lie;
A youth like thee for girl like her
Would fight till he did die.
"They've killed the lass," it was his tale,
"And nearly have killed me;"
But when upon him folks did look,
No bruises could they see."

ANDREW MILLS &
THE
MERRINGTON TRAGEDY

The murder of a whole family, the son and two daughters of John and Elizabeth Brass, took place in January 1683. Time may have distorted or embroidered some of the facts, but the tragic deaths of the young people caused such an outrage that they have been remembered to this day.

The Brass family owned a farm called Hill House in Merrington, near Bishop Auckland, Co. Durham. In 1683, John, the only son, was eighteen and helped his father on the farm. The account in the 'Monthly Chronicle' tells us he was a rather weak character who carried out his duties well enough but showed little initiative.

His elder sister, Jane, at twenty years old was a stronger character, who helped her mother with household duties, but having been courted by many of the local young men, was planning to marry soon. Her younger sister, Elizabeth, was eleven years old; a lively, cheeky but kind-hearted girl.

It was Elizabeth who was sympathetic and generous towards the servant lad, Andrew Mills. A simple minded youth in his late teens, he was normally quiet and inoffensive if left alone, but Mills could become violent if provoked and *"a dangerous light flashed from his usually dull eyes."* These fits of temper were infrequent, and never occurred with the good-humoured Elizabeth.

During earlier centuries, Christmas was celebrated for a much longer period of time in England, often two weeks or more. One evening, around the 26th or 28th January, the parents left their children at home, with Mills, and attended some festivities at a neighbour's house. Little did they know it was to be the last time they would see their family alive.

36

The only account of the terrible deeds which followed at the farm are those told by Mills in his later confession. He gave no motive for his crime, saying only that the devil told him to carry out the dreadful murders. We can only assume that something or someone triggered off this explosion of violence as Mills appeared to chase the young people into a particular room of the house before committing the gruesome crime. Surtees, in his 'History of Durham', suggests that Mills was jealous of Jane's forthcoming marriage, but there are no accounts to confirm this.

Undoubtedly John and Jane together should have been capable of restraining or overpowering the angered Mills, but it seems that the son, due to his weak character, stood by as the enraged servant forced them into a room in the house. Jane, however, was not prepared to give in easily and, frantic with horror and fear at finding herself trapped in the room, fought heroically to keep Mills out and bar the door.

There was no bolt but the brave girl put her arm through the bars of the door, holding off the incensed murderer for a short time. It is only just possible to imagine the extreme horror the girl must have experienced during the minutes it took Mills to break down the door, and, most dreadfully, break the girl's arm. Unable to provide further resistance, Jane, together with her brother, was murdered immediately.

Mills spared his favourite, Elizabeth, only moments longer as she cried for mercy. Innocently, she offered him food, her toys - anything if only he would spare her life. Slightly swayed by the force of her pleas, he left the bedroom, but the devil again urged him to "Kill all! Kill all!" Returning to the room, Mills dragged the girl from her hiding place under the bed and completed his evil task by "dashing at her brains."

There are several accounts as to what happened next. Some say Mills did not attempt to escape, but stayed with his victims until their parents returned, others that he escaped to Ferryhill, where his crazed appearance and wild talk resulted in his arrest. He was also said to have met the parents returning home on the exact spot where he was later to be gibbeted. The couple's horse was apparently terrified by the unearthly howls of dogs and the screeching of owls, and it refused to go any further. Mills was supposed to be seized here by troopers marching from Darlington to Durham.

No matter how he was eventually brought to justice, Andrew Mills was tried, executed and hung in chains on a common near Ferryhill. Mills' body would have hung there for some time according to the custom of the day, and it is for the gibbeting rather than for the murder that he became famous.

There are many stories connected with the gibbeting, as tradition claims he was hung alive. Mills' cries of agony, as his hunger increased and his life faded fast, echoed around the nearby villages, forcing people to leave their homes, returning only when the murderer finally gained his lasting peace. Some say his life was prolonged by a sweetheart feeding him milk through the iron cage. A more horrific version suggests that a loaf of bread was placed on a iron spike just within his reach; the spike entered his throat every time he attempted to eat!

These tales are, without doubt, untrue, but they built upon the legend of Andrew Mills with which mothers in Durham used to threaten their naughty children for decades to come. The gibbet, known as 'Andrew Mills's Stob', stood for many years and splinters of wood were taken by local people, believing that they would cure toothache. A monument in Merrington churchyard bore the following inscription:

"Here lie the Bodies of John, Jane and Elizabeth,
children of John and Margaret Brass,
who were murdered the 28th January, 1683,
by Andrew Mills, their father's servant,
for which he was executed and hung in chains."

HALF HANGED
MACDONALD

After the 1745 Jacobite Rebellion an agreement was made with the English government that Highland soldiers should serve exclusively in Scotland, more particularly the Highlands, in the role of a local militia. However, the government were often in breach of this agreement and the soldiers who were brought into England were subjected to taunts and jeers from their English neighbours.

One such Highlander was Ewan Macdonald, a nineteen year old youth serving with General Guise's regiment, the 43rd Royal Highlanders, who were quartered in Newcastle. At around ten o'clock on Tuesday 23rd March, 1752, Macdonald entered an inn owned by a Mr. Pinkney, in the Bigg Market, Newcastle.

The inn was full and the appearance of the soldier in full Highland dress uniform caused much jeering and rude jokes from the English revellers. Macdonald tolerated the jokes for a while, but then suddenly lost his patience and, rising from his seat, shaking with anger, he fought with one of the offenders.

The man, Parker, a cooper by trade, escaped the enraged soldier's grasp and ran out into the street. Robert Parker, another cooper much respected in his trade, had taken little part in the jibes, and prepared to leave, along with several others wanting to escape the wrath of the furious Highlander.

Bent on revenge, Macdonald pursued these runaways, and caught hold of Robert Parker in the doorway as he was leaving, and fatally stabbed him with a gully knife. Returning to the inn kitchen, *"black with passion"*, the young soldier began attacking other customers who had not yet escaped, breaking one person's arm.

Someone ran to the barracks and brought a group of soldiers who conducted Macdonald, mad with anger, to the guard house. He was confined there until the next day when he appeared before the magistrate and was committed to Newgate prison. A verdict of 'Guilty' was returned by the coroner's jury. When Macdonald appeared at the next Assizes, the charge of murder was conclusive. He was sentenced to death on the scaffold.

It is possible that today a charge of manslaughter would have been brought against the impulsive Highlander. Even public opinion of the time was that the justice dealt to Macdonald was somewhat unfair, as he was undoubtedly provoked into his ruthless action.

During his time in prison, Macdonald regretted his wild actions, particularly as Mr. Robert Parker had taken no real part in the foolish taunting. However, despite his repentance, Macdonald again acted rashly as he was brought to the scaffold and attempted to throw the executioner from the ladder. This action horrified the priest, the sheriff and his assistants.

After the execution, the body hung for what was thought to be a sufficient length of time and was then cut down to be taken to the Surgeon's Hall for dissection. As it was placed on the operating table, however, the surgeons were called away to the Infirmary.

On their return they were astonished and horrified to see that Macdonald had recovered sufficiently to be able to sit up and beg for mercy. There was to be none - a young surgeon, not wishing to miss the opportunity to dissect the body, struck Macdonald a fatal blow to the head with a wooden mallet. Sykes, in his 'Local Records', claims that a mallet put on show at the Surgeon's Hall was that used to kill Macdonald and that the surgeon who dealt the deadly blow was killed soon afterwards by his own horse in a stable.

WINTER'S GIBBET

A few miles from Elsdon, near Otterburn, among the wild Northumbrian moors, Winter's Gibbet stands starkly outlined against the sky. The famous gibbet, or stob, with its macabre wooden head, is a gruesome reminder of a terrible murder which took place nearby.

The tragic event occurred in 1791, the victim being an elderly woman, Margaret Crozier. She lived in part of an old peel house, Haws Peel at Raw and ran the local general shop, selling drapery and other goods. One Monday night, 29th August, two of her friends, Elizabeth Jackson, a farmer's daughter, and Mary Temple, an expert needlewoman, came to spend the evening with her.

A couple of hours later, as they prepared to leave, they heard the furious barking of two or three dogs around a pile of hay which lay nearby. Alarmed at this, the friends reminded Margaret to bolt her door for safety. She laughed, replying she *"had naething to fear, as nae doubt ane o' Bessie's sweethearts was no far off waiting to see her."* 'Bessie' being her friend, Elizabeth Jackson.

Next morning, as a customer, Barbara Drummond, arrived at the shop to make a purchase, she noticed some thread and other small items lying outside the shop doorway. Suspecting foul play, she hurried to tell some of the neighbours. Elizabeth Jackson and William Dodds, a joiner, not having seen Margaret that morning, rushed to her shop and opened the door.

A terrible sight awaited them : Margaret was lying on her bed, dead, with her throat cut.

Investigating further, they realised that the wound was hardly deep enough to have caused her death, and it was

41

bound up tightly with a handkerchief, suggesting that strangulation may have been the final cause of death.

The palm of one of her hands was severely lacerated, as if the old woman had fought desperately for her life. A blood stained gully knife (long butcher's knife) was found among the bedclothes. It became obvious that various articles of clothing, materials and other linen had been stolen.

The event, not surprisingly, caused a great amount of excitement and horror in such a quiet neighbourhood, and soon everyone regardless of class or position, was involved in the search for the murderer. A reward was offered for any information which might prove useful, and people were asked to report on strangers seen in the area.

Two boys came forward who had seen three people, a man and two women, acting suspiciously the day before the murder. The three suspects were resting and eating a meal at a sheepfold overlooking Margaret Crozier's house. The boys paid particular attention to the man who they described as tall and well-built, and one of the boys, Richard Hindmarsh, noticed a gully knife bound with an iron band to prevent it from splitting, which the man used to cut and divide the food. Hindmarsh was also able to observe the man's feet as he sat enjoying his meal, the boy remembered the type of nails in the bottom of his shoes.

This evidence was reported to the coroner who delayed the inquest until the young witnesses could appear. Hindmarsh, being the more observant of the two, related these facts, and having been shown the knife found at the scene of the murder, he identified it as that which the man had used to share the food. Footmarks found outside the house at Raw also corresponded to Hindmarsh's description.

Other local people who had seen the strangers then came forward, and it was discovered that the suspects had been later observed with a loaded ass near Harlow Hill. Some stolen raisins and peas were found near the pile of hay at the sheepfold which was a clue to the route the three had taken.

The man was described as nearly six feet tall, of a large powerful build, with long black hair tied at the back and he wore a light-coloured coat, blue breeches and grey stockings. The women were also tall and stout, wearing grey cloaks and black bonnets.

The local constables followed the clues and finally arrested the man, William Winter, near Horsley. The two women, sisters Jane and Eleanor Clark, were apprehended a little later at Ovingham and Barley Moor, respectively. They were all found to be connected to the 'Faw Gangs' or tribes of gypsies prevalent in Northumbria at one time.

The prisoners were then taken to Mitford to be examined by Mr. B. Mitford. Winter's shirt was found to be stained with blood, which he alleged had happened while fighting with another of his tribe. Mr. Mitford pointed out, however, that Winter would probably have removed his shirt if involved in such a fight. The suspicions confirmed against them, the three were committed to Morpeth gaol on 3rd September 1791.

As the assizes were only held once a year, the three remained in gaol until the following August, when their trial was held at the Moot Hall in Newcastle. It lasted sixteen hours and the strongest evidence was that given by the boys, concerning the knife and footprints. A friend of Mrs. Crozier's also identified a nightcap found in the possession of one of the accused women, as being one which she had made herself for the murdered woman.

The three prisoners were found guilty and were sentenced to be executed. Winter's body was to be hung in chains on a gibbet within sight of the scene of the murder, and the bodies of the two sisters would be sent to the Surgeon's Hall for dissection. On Friday morning, 10th August, 1792, they were hanged at Westgate, Winter having admitted his guilt, although the women still protested their innocence.

For some time Winter's body was left to hang on the gallows, and was then taken down and transported in a long cart to its final exposure on a gibbet at Steng Cross. Thousands were said to have witnessed this macabre event. As the body was so heavy, a set of shear legs (a device for lifting heavy weights) was borrowed to hoist it into position. The crowd dispersed, leaving the ghastly spectacle silhouetted against the sky.

Through time the body began to decay, the smell being so offensive that horses refused to pass the gibbet. The clothes rotted away and the loose bones were eventually hung in a new sack, tarred inside to resist the weather on the exposed moors. As this too decayed, the whitened remains fell to the ground and were buried by local shepherds. When the last mortal remains had disappeared, a wooden figure of a man was hung from the gibbet, but it too finally succumbed to the ravages of time and exposure to the elements. Local people who believed that splinters of wood from the effigy cured toothache, precipitated its destruction.

Around 1867, Sir Walter Trevelyan of Wallington Hall, ordered a new gibbet to be built on the spot, and a wooden head, reputedly painted in lurid colours, was hung from the arm.

This head remained in place for many years until recently when it was subject to more modern methods of destruction as it was stolen, and the gibbet vandalised. In April 1989 a ceremony was held at the site to hang a replacement head carved by Alan Urwin, a worker on the Wallington Estate.

Although the murder of Maragret Crozier took place almost 200 years ago, and Winter's body has long since decayed, the lasting reminder of Winter's Stob will continue to be regarded with a hint of suspicion and awe.

THE LAST GIBBET IN ENGLAND

The last gibbet to be erected in England was reputedly at Jarrow Slake, near South Shields, and it was demolished in September 1856 by workmen who were constructing Tyne Dock for the North Eastern Railway Company. William Jobling, a thirty year old pitman accused of murdering a South Shields magistrate, Nicholas Fairles, was the last offender to hang in chains on the gibbet.

Mr. Fairles was murdered during the 1832 pitmen's strike which caused much bitterness and ill-feeling between the pitmen and their employers. Hundreds of families were turned out of their cottages and for months had to camp out in lanes and at the road side. Soldiers and special constables were on guard outside the collieries to prevent the angry pitmen from gaining entry.

Three murders were committed by the pitmen during this turbulent time. The county magistrate, Nicholas Fairles, was one of those victims.

At around five o'clock on the 11th June he was riding around Jarrow Slake from his own home in South Shields, towards Jarrow Colliery in another attempt to maintain law and order at the pit. Suddenly he was stopped by two pitmen, apparently begging for money, when one of them seized his leg and pulled him from his horse.

They dealt Mr. Fairles a violent blow to the head, knocking him unconscious. Not content with this, they kicked and beat the magistrate, finally leaving his almost lifeless body at the roadside. Someone from a nearby house saw the incident and ran to help Mr. Fairles but due to the particularly severe wounds to his head, the magistrate died ten days later on 21st June.

One of the men, Jobling, was immediately arrested the same night of the attack. His companion, however, Ralph Armstrong, escaped and was never seen again. A £400 reward notice was issued by Lord Melbourne from Whitehall for anyone knowing the whereabouts of Armstrong.

At the coroner's inquest, held at Mr. Oyston's inn in South Shields, surgeons were examined along with witnesses to the incident. The jury returned a verdict of 'Guilty' against Jobling, and the absent Armstrong.

The funeral of Mr. Fairles took place on 27th June and, with the flags at half-mast and most of the shops closed, a procession of dignitaries led by the Mayor and Sheriff of Newcastle together with many local people, marched solemnly through South Shields. The magistrate's coffin was made from a tree, originally planted when Mr. Fairles had come of age.

William Jobling was tried and found guilty of murder and was sentenced to be hanged at Durham on Friday 3rd August 1832, his body to later hang in chains near the scene of the crime. The old law concerning gibbeting had recently been revived and Jobling was believed to be the only person gibbeted under the Act until it was later repealed.

Jobling accepted his sentence but denied being the principal partner in the crime. As the day of execution was particularly wet, there was not such a huge crowd at Durham and fifty of the 8th Hussars and fifty of the 15th Regiment of Foot were on hand until the body was cut down. They would later escort the body to Jarrow. Jobling mounted the steps to the scaffold steadily but was unable to address spectators as he intended to do, the power of speech having failed him.

As the final bolt was about to be withdrawn, one of the crowd shouted *"Farewell Jobling!"* Jobling turned his head in the direction of the cry and unfortunately moved the rope which resulted in prolonging his suffering. After hanging for an hour the body was cut down and taken into the gaol until the gibbet was ready. Jobling's clothes were removed as his body was covered in pitch and then reclothed.

At seven o'clock on Monday morning, 6th of August, the body was taken from Durham in a small waggon escorted by the soldiers and various officials, arriving at Jarrow Slake about half past one. Again, there were few spectators as the pitmen were holding a meeting at nearby Boldon.

The following description comes from the 'Monthly Chronicle' of 1888:

"The body was encased in flat bars of iron of $2^1/_2$ inches in breadth. The feet were placed in stirrups, from which a bar of iron went up each side of the head, and ended in a ring by which the corpse was suspended. A bar from the collar went down the breast, and another down the back. There were also bars on the inside of the legs which communicated with the above, and cross bars at the ankles, the knees, the thighs, the bowels, the breasts, and the shoulders. The hands were hung at the sides, and were covered with pitch. The face was pitched and covered with a piece of white cloth."

The corpse was then transported on a hand barrow at low tide, across the mud to the gibbet and erected almost directly opposite the scene of the crime. The gibbet was held in a stone weighing about one and half tons which was sunk in the mud and was made from a piece of fir timber, twenty one feet long, with a top piece projecting about three feet with strong iron bars covering each side to prevent it from being sawn down. At high tide about four or five feet of the gibbet was covered, leaving almost seventeen feet above the water, ensuring that the body was always visible. The corpse was then hoisted into place and the police remained on guard for quite some time.

Three weeks later, however, on a moonless night, between 31st August and 1st September, the body was removed. It was believed to have been taken by Jobling's fellow pitmen and was either buried at sea or under the walls of the monastery at Jarrow.

ORDEAL BY FIRE
THE MURDER ON OTTERBURN MOOR

More than 60 years ago, on a bleak January night there took place in Northumberland, a particularly horrific and fatal attack on a young woman. It appeared from the evidence of the time that she was stunned and the car in which she sat was then fired. Surviving only a short time because of extensive burns, her last words were : *"I have been murdered."*

The unfortunate victim was Evelyn Foster, aged 27, the daughter of the owner of a local transport company. On the night in question, according to the somewhat garbled story she told after her rescue, the following incidents took place.

As an experienced and competent driver, she often handled the hire-car part of her father's business. The previous day she had driven three passengers to Rochester, and at Eilshaw on her return journey, was stopped by a man who wanted to go to Ponteland to meet a connection to Newcastle. Evelyn arranged to pick him up at the Percy Arms Hotel, but when she arrived there he was not in sight. Driving on, she recognised the man, stopped, and then proceeded with her passenger to Newcastle.

Just past Belsay he suddenly yelled at her to stop, and when she asked why, he punched her viciously in the face, and began to wrestle her for control of the car. He eventually took over the wheel and heading towards Otterburn, suddenly swung the car off the road, down a steep bank and across the moor at 'Wolf's Neck'.

To Evelyn's horror the man suddenly stopped the car, leapt out and seemed to pull something from his pocket to which he set light, causing a burst of flames and a small explosion. Coughing and choking from the flames and frantically trying to extinguish her burning clothes, Evelyn

48

crawled and fell from the car. She was vaguely aware of her attacker striding off in the distance towards the road.

In agony from her terrible burns she fell face downwards on the ground, and thankfully licked at some icy puddles in the grass to try and quench her thirst. She must have fainted as the next thing she remembered was the arrival of Mr. Johnson.

As an employee of Foster's transport, Mr. Johnson had been driving his bus along the road, when he saw the burning wreck in the distance. He and his conductor carried the badly injured girl to their vehicle wrapped in a coat and then drove her home as fast as possible. During the journey Evelyn was heard to murmur several times as in a delirium, *"Oh that awful man. He has gone in a motor car. Oh that awful man."*

Tragically Eveyln survived only long enough to relate her horrific story, and then died from burns and shock. The whole district were appalled by this fiendishly murderous attack on a young innocent woman. The police were alerted and a warning issued that a dangerous lunatic was at large. Miss Foster's bag was found intact, and there was no evidence of any sexual interference, thus ruling out the obvious motives.

A description was pieced together from Evelyn's story and circulated. The man was aged about 25, 5′ 6″ tall; clean-shaven, wearing a dark tweed suit, bowler hat and overcoat. He spoke in a well-educated manner with a Tyneside accent. In spite of the best efforts of the police he was never found.

A coroner's inquest was opened on Thursday 8th January at the Ottershaw Memorial Hall, where evidence was given by Evelyn's parents and the police. After an adjournment for police enquiries, the inquest re-opened on 5th February. The post-mortem results were given by Professor Stuart McDonald from Durham University.

"The features were obscured by burns, but there appeared to be discoloration about the root of the nose. Extensive burns were distributed about various parts of the body. An internal examination showed no injury except severe burning. From these appearances we

[the post-mortem was carried out with the assistance of Dr. McEachran] *are of the opinion that the cause of death was shock, the result of severe external burning. The distribution of the burns and their severity suggest that certain portions of the clothing had contained some inflammable substance. The distribution of the burned areas suggests that Miss Foster was sitting during some period of the burning. The situation of other burns indicates that there had been splashes of an inflammable liquid."*

Professor McDonald then stated that although Eveylyn Forster claimed to have been punched, there was no evidence of bruising on her face. At this point in the inquest, the coroner, Mr. P. M. Dodds, put a question to the witness which was to cast the most controversial doubt.

"Assuming the car was where you saw it, and she threw some petrol into the back of the car and set fire to it, with her left leg probably on the running board and her right on the edge of the step, could the flames have come back and blinded her?"

A hushed courtroom heard the considered reply from the Professor : *"I think it quite possible."*

From this statement questions were raised as to the truth of Evelyn's account of her attack, so that when the judge delivered his speech to the jury, they were asked to consider whether the girl was murdered, or had she done it herself. Could her objective have been to claim insurance for the car (as much at £450)?

After considering the case, the jury returned a verdict of murder *"by person or persons unknown"*. Although this outcome brought relief to all concerned, Evelyn's father, Mr. Foster, was still dissatisfied. He sent a strongly worded letter of complaint to the Home Secretary in which he made it clear how much he resented the suggestion that his daughter may have set fire to the car herself.

Essentially though, the whole episode remains a mystery. Who but a homicidal maniac would have perpetrated such a crime? With what possible motive, and for what possible gain?

TRAGEDY
AT URPETH MILL

The following tragedy unfolded at Urpeth, also known as Hutchinsons, corn mill at Urpeth on the Team Valley, Gateshead. The calm idyllic scene of this beautiful wooded valley was shattered on Saturday 29th September 1860, as a woman ran screaming from the cottage adjoining the mill, shouting *"Murder!"*

Mrs. Lockey was being pursued by her husband, Milner Lockey, from whom she was now separated on the grounds of his cruelty. Lockey had moved away to work at Leasingthorn Colliery, near Bishop Auckland, but decided to pay his wife an unwelcome visit. He had become insanely jealous when he heard that she had recently taken in a lodger, Mr. Bell, to help her financially and he began to believe that she was intimately involved with him. Lockey made frequent unwanted visits to the house and his jealousy grew to such an extent that he planned to kill his wife, and then himself.

It was with this in mind that he set out for the mill on 29th September, stopping on the way for a glass of whisky with some friends. It seems he hinted to his companions of his murderous intentions, and presumably fired up by the whisky, carried on to the cottage.

Arriving around 7 o'clock, Lockey was greeted warily by his wife who asked what he was doing in her home. *"You'll find out before lang"* was the sneering reply. Having verbally abused his wife, Lockey took a knife, recently purchased, from his pocket and shrieked *"thou'll not be lang here"* and struck Mrs. Lockey on the chest. The knife bounced off the bone in her corset and he struck her again, with the same result. Wild with anger and determined to kill her, he aimed the knife at her bowels but fortunately it only entered her thigh.

Mrs. Lockey's eleven year old son by a previous marriage, Samuel Wilson, was disturbed from his bed by the noise and came down to beg Lockey to leave his mother alone. The lodger, asleep on the kitchen floor, also tried to restrain Lockey, but the mad man, thinking that the blow to his wife had been fatal, turned on the poor man and plunged the knife into his left breast. He fell to the floor, dead.

Meanwhile the boy had rushed from the house to get help at the Ridings Farm. Sobbing and crying he told his terrible tale of the events at the cottage and two of the farm hands, Wright and Hart, returned with him to the mill.

As they approached, Mrs. Lockey, having taken the knife from her husband, was escaping, closely followed by Lockey, furious that he had not dealt her a fatal blow. Unfortunately the two farm hands did not attempt to stop Lockey and the pursuit continued. Pushing herself to the limits, Mrs. Lockey raced up a hill and into a field of barley, out of sight from her husband.

By this time two police officers had arrived from Chester-le-Street and a description of the murderer was circulated to other forces in the county. A search of the area began and at half past five the following morning, thanks to the farm hands having followed Lockey, he was discovered hiding in a pig sty near Urpeth.

Lockey was tried at Durham and sentenced to death, showing no signs of remorse for his crime. At nine o'clock on a bitterly cold day, December 27th 1860, the execution took place in front of the county court at Durham. Hundreds watched the event and thousands were seen on the road leading to the City

MYSTERIOUS
MURDER AT STREETGATE

Following the annual flower show held on 28th August 1865, the young people of Streetgate and the surrounding area danced to a local band in a marquee pitched on the Ravensworth Estate in Gateshead. Little did they know that this was to be their last flower show dance and that one of their companions would be murdered before the day ended.

As the dancers enjoyed themselves a loud argument was taking place in the kitchen of the nearby Marquis of Granby Inn, much to the annoyance of the landlord, William Laidman. A group of men, including the outside servants from Ravensworth Castle, a little the worse for drink, were engaged in a ferocious quarrel and loud threats were overheard, the worst against a Joseph Leybourne.

The quarrel originated over Leybourne taking the side of a young farm worker from Hexham called Nixon, against a notorious character and wandering cobbler, Jack Bee.

The feud continued until closing time which had been extended because of the flower show. A female witness who lived a few doors away from the Inn, claimed the men emerged from the pub at two o'clock on the Tuesday morning, cursing and swearing, and one voice was heard threatening Joseph Leybourne, declaring he would *"knock his soul out."*

The witness, scenting danger, called all her relatives into the house as the gang made their way up the hill to Sunniside. It was out on this dark lonely road that a foul murder took place and *"as they slunk away to their several homes, their number was one less."*

The dance now over, most people were making their way home, and one of the last to come up the hill was a respected villager, George Mudd. Accompanied by some other men and carrying a lamp in his hand, he had not gone far when a friend called his attention to a man sitting on a stone propped up against the hedge.

Assuming he was drunk, the men called out but received no reply. As George Mudd shone his lamp on the figure, the light revealed the ghastly and blood-stained face of a dead man, instantly recognisable as Joseph Leybourne. He had sustained two wounds to his head and the light revealed blood on the stones nearby. Later a heavy sharp stone, covered with blood and hairs, was found in a neighbouroughing field.

The men made a makeshift stretcher and slowly carried the battered body of Joseph Leybourne to his home. Hoping to break the news gently to his wife, they shouted that Joe had been hurt but it seems his wife had a premonition of the impending disaster and replied *"No, he has not been hurt, he is dead.."*

It was never revealed who had committed the evil deed. A report of the adjourned inquest appeared in the 'Newcastle Daily Chronicle' of Friday, 22nd September, 1865, and a verdict of 'wilful murder' was brought against some person or persons unknown.

The local policeman, Miles Robinson, known as Miley, assisted by other members of the force, searched the area for enough evidence to bring someone to trial. Many were examined and a few suspected and it was said that had not the respected Mr. Mudd vouched for the men with him on the fatal night, they too may have been suspected.

Lord Ravensworth, in order to clear the good name of the castle, was so appalled that such a terrible deed had taken place on his estate that he promptly dismissed all the men servants who had been in the Marquis of Granby that night. He also gave instructions that no more flower shows were to be held at Streetgate - certainly not in his lifetime and not without his permission. Trade at the Marquis of Granby also suffered as people were afraid to go near in case they too were regarded as potential suspects.

So what of the infamous Jack Bee? Originally from Cumberland, but at the time of the murder 'of no fixed abode', he remained the most likely suspect but insufficient evidence meant that he could not be brought to trial. Shortly before his death he was overheard in a public house declaring that while he was not responsible for Leybourne's murder, he did know who had struck the fatal blow but swore that he would not reveal the name.

Some people who knew Bee remembered him as *"a tall muscular, swash-buckler kind of character"*, and they stated that although he was a bit of a rough diamond, he would always defend the underdog. Although this may have been true, as everyone has their good points, he does seem to have been *"a character of somewhat bad repute."*

It is more than likely that he did have a hand in the killing of Joseph Leybourne and it was rumoured that the morning after the killing, Bee, a shrewd man and more than capable of evading the law, spoke privately to each member of the gang who most likely led Leybourne to his death. Could it be that he threatened and struck such terror into each man for them to keep silent ? The mystery has never been solved.

NEWGATE STREET STABBING

Here we have a tale of terrible conflict between two of Northumberland's most ancient and important families: the Fenwicks and the Forsters.

The Forsters rose to prominence when James I gave them the manor and castle of Bamburgh, which they later lost during the 1715 Jacobite Rebellion. With their family seat at Wallington the Fenwicks, of Saxon origin, were famous in Border Legend and were looked on by the House of Percy as their favourite retainers.

In 1701, John Fenwick, then living at Rock Hall, near Alnwick, was summoned to appear on the Grand Jury at the Summer Assizes in Newcastle. Ferdinando Forster, Member of Parliament for Northumberland, was also called to the same service.

On 22nd August the Grand Jury dined at the Black Horse Inn. These banquets were traditionally regarded as an occasion where country gentlemen met together and plotted and brooded over the politics of the day. Ferdinando Forster, however, was one of the least quarrelsome, a man proud of his name and his ancient lineage, whereas Fenwick appears to have had quite an opinion of himself. Three years earlier Sir John Fenwick, known to have Jacobite sympathies, had been hanged at Tower Hill for plotting to kill the King. This, together with family quarrels over land or some other grudge, rankled between the two men.

On this particular day in August,1701, John Fenwick swaggered arrogantly into the room at the Inn singing *"Sir John Fenwick's the flower among them"* indicating that the Fenwicks were better than any other Northern family.

It seems that Forster took this as a personal insult and threw it back in Fenwick's face. As the two men faced each other angrily across the room, swords half-drawn, the rest of the company held them apart before they could attack each other.

There are two versions of what took place next. One is that on the intervention of their friends, the two men pretended that the matter was over and that the threats were not serious. However, on meeting each other by chance, the next day in Newgate Street, angry words were exchanged between the two and a sword fight ensued. It appears that Forster was killed as Fenwick *"fled for his life"*.

Another account states that a challenge to a duel was issued at the Inn. Forster led the way outside, with Fenwick and the rest of the company following on behind. When they were almost at the White Cross (removed in 1808) in Newgate Street, Fenwick, seized by uncontrollable rage, stabbed Forster in the back - a murder had been committed.

Fenwick escaped and hid in a garden in Gallowgate where he was soon captured and returned for trial. Another version states that Fenwick became a fugitive and it was some time before he was captured.

Whichever account one chooses to believe - that the deed was a cold-blooded murder or standup fight - the fact remains that a man was killed by Fenwick's hand.

Having appeared before the Assizes, which were still sitting, and put on trial before the judge with whom, only a few days earlier, he was on equal terms, Fenwick was found guilty and sentenced to be hanged. This was, indeed, rough justice if a duel had taken place but the only outcome if a cowardly stabbing resulted in murder.

Fearing a rescue attempt for Fenwick by the pitmen he employed at his Kenton colliery, the town gates were kept closed until after the execution.

According to the custom of the day, a scaffold was built near the town gate and within sight of the scene of the crime. On September 25th, John Fenwick was hung from these gallows for the murder of Ferdinando Forster.

STAND
AND DELIVER!

The famous cry of the highwayman reminds everyone of the unscrupulous Dick Turpin and his horse Black Bess. Northumberland and Durham also had their share of these reckless criminals, chancing their lives to escape with money, gold or jewels.

One such rogue named Hazlitt, although his real name was Hudson, had once been employed as a clerk in London. Having lost that job, he thought he might fare better in the north, and arrived at Shields in July 1770.

He looked, without success, for employment, and by the end of the first week had used all his remaining money to hire a horse, described as 'a sorry jade'. It is possible that Hazlitt had to leave his coat and boots as a deposit, as he was not wearing them during the crime which took place later on Gateshead Fell.

As the names implies, the Fell was once a wild common on the road between Durham and Newcastle. The loneliness of the bleak, dark moor frightened many a traveller over a century and a half ago.

On a particular day in July 1770, around dusk, a wealthy lady was returning to Newcastle from Durham in her post chaise after completing some business in the cathedral city. Suddenly her journey was abruptly brought to a halt, and looking out of the window, she saw to her horror, Hazlitt, brandishing a pistol. Opening the door of the chaise, he held the pistol at the lady's head while demanding her purse, watch and other portable valuables.

Hazlitt was, in fact, trembling from head to foot with excitement and, possibly, fear. Observing this, the lady explained that she did not have a watch and that she had spent most of her money in Durham except for a half guinea and a few pence. Hazlitt took the half guinea, generously leaving the few coppers and, although surprised there was no watch, took the lady's word for it, and left.

After going a mile or so on her journey, she met the postman on horseback and told him of the danger which may be waiting for him, urging that he either turn back or arm himself. He refused to turn back, and although he was unable to get a pistol at the toll house, decided to carry on despite the risks.

The postman shortly caught up with a man on horseback who he took to be a peasant returning from a day's labour. He began to tell the worker about the highwayman who may be waiting somewhere on the desolate moor, and confessed that he was unarmed. They continued to chatter for about another mile or so, when the 'peasant' suddenly asked, in a quiet voice, for the mail bags. The postman thought it was a joke until Hazlitt produced his pistol and ordered the man to dismount and throw the mail on the road. Fearing for his life, the postman did as he was told. Hazlitt then took the mail off to a lonely spot to examine it for bills and letters which he could convert into cash.

About an hour or two later Hazlitt made another attempt at holding up a post chaise belonging to a Mr. Nelson from Newcastle. It was found to be empty, however, and not worth the trouble. It seems that Hazlitt then went on to Newcastle rather than returning to Shields, and was arrested there the next day in possession of the valuable contents of the mail bags.

He was brought to trial at the Durham Assizes within a week and pleaded guilty to robbing the lady in the post chaise. On the advice of the judge, he changed his plea to 'not guilty', but was convicted of the crime. He pleaded not guilty to the charge of robbing the postman, but after two hours the outrage against his crimes was made plain, and according to the harsh law of the time, he was sentenced to death.

When Hazlitt gave his own version of events he stated that an associate, Hewitt, had stolen the mail which they then shared between them. It was discovered later that Hewitt was in London at the time of the crime, and the execution was set to go ahead.

On Tuesday, 18th September, Hazlitt was hanged near Durham, and after hanging some time, the body was cut down and taken to Gateshead Fell where a gibbet had been erected. It was there it hung in chains. Other robberies with violence were said to have been committed in the area while the body was in the early stages of decay. The daring highwayman was recalled long after in the name of 'Hazlitt's Well'.

At a much later date, September 1821, two 'notorious' highwaymen, Wilkinson and Hetherington, were executed at Morpeth. During their lives both men had little education and soon fell into a life of crime. John Wilkinson was born around 1787 and as a boy worked with his father in various pits.

When he was about thirty years old, he worked at St. Hilda's pit, near South Shields. One day he was given a parcel of bank notes, about £12 or £13, to pay himself and his fellow workers. The temptation was too great and he escaped with the money and although arrested, there was not enough evidence against him and he was released. His work mates took the law into their own hands, and having stripped, tarred and feathered Wilkinson, threw him into a pond near the pit.

Wilkinson moved to Sunderland, taking on various jobs, but fell in with unsavoury characters and began to follow a life of crime. Suspected of being involved in various robberies, he was arrested on 19th May, 1821, together with Thomas Dodds. They were charged with robbing an Irish labourer, Paul Riggen, on the Ponteland Road, of his silver watch, key, seals and ten shillings (50p), tried at Northumberland Assizes on 25th August and found guilty.

Three days later, another member of the gang, William Surtees Hetherington, together with Wilkinson, were put on trial for a highway robbery, the previous 7th April.

Hetherington, also the son of a miner, was born in Newburn in 1789 and, having spent six years at sea, led a vagrant life, before finally resorting to crime. Hetherington was detained on several charges, including the robbery of William Nesbit, a farmer from Longbenton.

The farmer had left Newcastle market one Saturday at about quarter to nine, carrying a pocket book containing two £5 notes and four £1 notes. As he was half way up Benton Bank, three men sprang out from the side of a wall, Wilkinson, Hetherington and a third man, Maddison. Mr. Nesbit was dragged from his horse, beaten and left unconscious at the side of the road.

The three highwaymen then went to the Grey Horse Inn on the quayside to examine their stolen prize. They managed to change the two £5 notes in the Sandhill by purchasing a hat and a bottle of rum. Going across to Gateshead to another inn, they divided the rest of the money between them.

For this outrageous crime, the three received the death sentence, although Maddison was later reprieved. Wilkinson and Hetherington awoke early on the day of execution, both hoping that their sentence would also be commuted to transportation. It was not to be. They were taken to Low Stanners, Morpeth, the place of execution, and Hetherington was later buried at Newburn, and Wilkinson at Jarrow.